GUESS THE COVERED WORD

FOR FOURTH GRADE

by
Joyce Kohfeldt
Helen S. Collier

Editor

Joey Bland

Table of Contents

KEY

B = words found at the **beginning** of sentences
M = words found in the **middle** of sentences
E = words found at the **end** of sentences
* = lesson written in paragraph(s)
PLUS: a list of initial consonants, blends, and
    digraphs for each covered word in the lesson

Introduction

By fourth grade most students have become independent readers who can meet the challenges of reading in all content areas, such as reading maps and diagrams in social studies, encountering terms like "respiration" in science, and reading charts, graphs, and new words like "quotient" in math. There has been a major shift from learning to read to reading to learn, so students must have their strategies in good working order. There is no time to sound out each new word. Comprehension becomes more essential as students are expected to use critical thinking skills and a higher level of analysis, and to apply the information they read. Without a consistent system for decoding the many new complex, content-specific words, a fourth grader can lose the motivation to learn, which leads to lower achievement.

Successful students this age enjoy reading alone, with a partner, in a small group like a literature circle, or with the whole class in a choral reading. Fourth graders still enjoy a teacher read-aloud. Their free-time reading choices include picture books geared for older students like *Barefoot: Escape on the Underground Railroad* by Pamela Edwards (HarperCollins Children's Books, 1997) or some of the *Magic School Bus* books by Joanna Cole. They enjoy nonfiction books, and are fascinated by the wonders of nature. Most fourth graders enjoy novels by a wide range of authors, like Judy Blume or C. S. Lewis. Others choose multi-cultural versions of *Cinderella*, such as *Mufaro's Beautiful Daughters* by John Steptoe (William Morrow & Co., 1988) or *Yeh Shen: A Cinderella Story from China* by Ai-Ling Louie (Putnam Publishing Group, 1982).

What does Guess the Covered Word have to offer this variety of fourth grade students with varying interests and skill levels? Reading, like learning to ski, is a skill that requires a range of prerequisites, many instructional opportunities, a range of practice and integration time, and ongoing assessment and monitoring. Reading and skiing are both tasks that different individuals master at different ages, and to differing degrees of proficiency.

When mastering skiing you cannot sit beside the slopes and practice walking with skis on one day, bending your knees to turn on the weekend, and balancing next week. These necessary components to skiing cannot be mastered in isolation or in any place other than on the ski slopes. The novice skier, whatever the age might be, starts on a beginner slope with close supervision. After mastering the basics, the skier moves to steeper slopes and faster runs. Soon, skiing has become a great hobby or a skill that may even lead to a related occupation.

Reading too is a complex skill. You cannot practice phonics on worksheets some days, comprehension questions from a book on some days, and other isolated vocabulary development activities on still other days. **You cannot practice and apply the skills just during reading time. You must see how to transfer them to science, social studies, and math class.**

Guess the Covered Word offers students at any age a cross-checking strategy that combines comprehension, context clues, and phonics. The examples, instruction, and practice of the Guess the Covered Word strategy appear in science, social studies, general themes, and math, as well as with a literature connection.

Learning to read is a complex task that requires a variety of skills, experience and practice. Reading requires the following:

- comprehension, thinking, and processing meaning (Students must expect print to make sense and must perceive the reader's job to include rereading and self-correcting when the text, as it is being read, fails to make sense.)

- visual discrimination and the understanding of print concepts (speech bubbles; north, south, east, and west on a map; horizontal and vertical axes on a graph; or a cutaway diagram in science)

- visual and auditory skills of recognizing letter patterns and groupings like prefixes and suffixes, developing a visual sense for sounds that have more than one spelling pattern (hair and hare; there, their, and they're)

- knowing what to do when you bump into an unknown word while reading instead of randomly guessing
- utilizing both illustration and text to explore the full meaning of what is being read

Some fourth graders read along without difficulty when meeting words that are part of their sight vocabularies. **When they bump into an unknown word, however, they may resort to one of the following:**

- **They may stop in their tracks and look up at the teacher with a "rescue me" expression on their faces.** They stop being problem solvers and look to an "outside expert" for assistance. They either do not know (or choose not to use) any independent strategies. These readers are most at risk because they do not know how to proceed without an adult present.

- **They may try to sound out the word, letter by letter, and then blend the sounds back into a word.** In some cases this will work (c-a-t...cat). Many letter combinations, however, form sounds that are different from the sum of their individual letter sounds (c-h-a-r-t...ch-ar-t; s-t-a-t-i-o-n... st-a-tion). These readers use a "phonics only" approach that does not always work in English.

- **They may make a wild guess, substituting any word under the sun without expecting it to make sense.** This is not only a poor habit to form as a reader, but it also disrupts the flow of comprehension.

- **They may ask themselves, "What would make sense?" and substitute that word for the unknown word without looking carefully at the letters in the word or using phonics.** For these students, the flow of comprehension is left intact, but they do not develop the skills of decoding new words independently. When the new words they meet are in contexts of which they have little or no prior knowledge, this strategy will not work.

- **They may look at the word's beginning sound and say any word that starts with that sound.** They do not consider the other letters in the word or if the word makes sense in the context in which it was found. This strategy also leads to major disruption in the flow of comprehension since these "off the wall" substitutions seldom make sense.

The Guess the Covered Word strategy is a more systematic and comprehensive strategy than those just described. Guess the Covered Word is a cross-checking strategy that combines context clues, comprehension, phonics, and word analysis skills to decode unknown words. It teaches the student to ask three basic questions when confronting new words:

1. **What makes sense?**

2. **How long is the word?**

3. **How does the word begin (up to the first vowel)? Are there any prefixes, suffixes, or known "little" words, and what are all the other letters in the word?**

If you have been using the Four-Blocks™ Literacy Model developed by Patricia M. Cunningham and Dorothy P. Hall, then Guess the Covered Word will not be new to you. The four blocks described in their balanced literacy model include Guided Reading, Self-Selected Reading, Writing, and Working with Words. The Working with Words block for upper grades contains several strategies and activities that promote both reading and spelling. Nifty Thrifty Fifty is a strategy that focuses on more complex words with prefixes and suffixes. Guess the Covered Word is also one of the reading strategies introduced. It is a cross-checking strategy that combines context clues, comprehension, phonics, and word analysis skills to unlock new words. The strategy may be found in several publications, such as *The Teacher's Guide to the Four-Blocks™* by Patricia M. Cunningham, Dorothy P. Hall, and Cheryl Sigmon; *Month-by-Month Phonics for Upper Grades* by Patricia M. Cunningham and Dorothy P. Hall; *Word Wall "Plus" for Third Grade* by Patricia M. Cunningham, Dorothy P. Hall, and Joyce Kohfeldt; and *Phonics They Use* by Patricia M. Cunningham.

Regardless of whether or not you have been using the Four-Blocks™ Literacy Model, Guess the Covered Word will help your students know what to do when they are reading and bump into a word they do not know. **This resource was written to support any teacher working with students in fourth grade, ESL students who are older, or elementary studentsPwith special needs who are reading at about the fourth grade level.**

- The themes and topics were selected to be consistent with those taught in fourth grade classrooms across the country.

- The interest level of early fluent readers (eight and nine years old) influenced each lesson, including the chosen literature.

- **The high-frequency words include compounds** like "rainfall" and "bookstore," **words with prefixes** such as "explored" and "include," and **words with suffixes** like "amusing" and "plentiful." Also included are **homophones** like "site/sight" and "heard/herd," as well as **words often misspelled by students** such as "because" and "people." There are even **longer, more sophisticated words** like "scrumptious" and "evacuations."

- The content-specific words have been listed in the appendix (pages 60-63) to point out the richness in vocabulary opportunities in the selections.

- The examples come from real classrooms and were field tested with real students.

- The lessons represent a wide range of challenges for fourth graders. Easier lessons involve using sentences with the covered words in the middle, or at the end of the sentences. These examples will support the learning of at-risk readers and those who are being introduced to the strategy for the first time in fourth grade. Other examples are more challenging, with previously unexplored topics, lessons written in paragraphs, and more

of the covered words in the middle and beginning of the sentences.

- Examples of possible guesses made by students in fourth grade have been included in the appendix (pages 60-63). The range of these words, as well as the range of guesses you are likely to hear from your own students, will illustrate how Guess the Covered Word challenges the full spectrum of learners in any fourth grade.

Teachers from across the country often voice their difficulty in finding time to do everything they need to do. In a balanced literacy program there is direct instruction in both reading and writing. Students also have opportunities to apply what they have learned as they read and write. The ability of students to unlock new words as they read, and spell new words as they write, plays an integral part in a balanced program. Guess the Covered Word is an essential cross-checking reading strategy that uses the best brain research, comprehension context clues, word analysis, and phonics.

> This resource, *Guess the Covered Word for Fourth Grade*, provides examples to show how the strategy of Guess the Covered Word can be used throughout the day and applied in multiple content areas and settings.

GUESS THE COVERED WORD CAN BE USED IN THESE AREAS:

- **Social Studies**, where students are reading and meeting new content words like "communities" and "map compass."

- **Science**, where lots of new words like "camouflage" or "tornadoes" pop up and challenge young readers.

- **Math**, where students are exposed to many words like "quotient" or "denominator" which are not part of their everyday listening or speaking vocabularies.

- **Themes** or units, where new words like "consumer" or "spreadsheet" might surface.

- **Literature Links** within a read aloud or literature circle contact where students come in contact with new words found in a novel.

GENERAL DIRECTIONS FOR TEACHING A GUESS THE COVERED WORD LESSON

Guess the Covered Word lessons have more than one level of difficulty based on the level of phonics/structural analysis knowledge needed, the placement of the covered word in the sentence, and whether simple sentences versus longer, complex sentences or paragraphs are used for context. The easiest lessons are covered words that begin with a single consonant, while more advanced lessons contain covered words with blends, digraphs, and prefixes.

The easiest lessons also have the covered word located at the end of a sentence. More advanced lessons may have the covered word located in the middle of the sentence, while sentences with the covered word at the beginning are the most difficult. If the word is in the middle or near the beginning of a sentence, another step will be added to the procedure. **That extra step involves making an "mmm" sound when you come to the covered word and putting your finger on the covered word as a place keeper.** The rest of the sentence must also be read in order to pick up as many clues as possible before asking, "What makes sense?"

Easier lessons also use simple sentences, while more advanced lessons may include covered words in longer, more complex sentences or within a paragraph. It is easier for students to use the Guess the Covered Word strategy with simple sentences than in a paragraph, where information or clues from earlier sentences may be useful or necessary to determine the covered word.

The Table of Contents contains information about the difficulty level of each lesson. You can select examples written as sentences or paragraphs, as well as examples with covered words in the beginning, middle, end, or all three.

By fourth grade, most students should be able to meet the challenge of words that begin with consonants, blends, digraphs, or prefixes. If this is your students' first exposure to the strategy, consider starting with simple sentences where many of the covered words appear at the ends of sentences.

TEACHER PREPARATION

- Choose a Guess the Covered Word example from a ready-to-use transparency or copy a black-and-white example onto a transparency.

Shopping for holiday gifts on the Internet can be an interesting experience.

- Use sticky notes or small pieces of paper (easily stored in a plastic bag for continuous use) to cover the bold words in the lesson. If the word to be covered begins with a consonant, digraph, or blend, use a separate sticky note to cover those consonants (onset) that come before the first vowel. Use another sticky note to cover the rest of the word (rime), beginning with the vowel. Cut or tear the sticky notes to be only as long as the word since word length is one of the strategy steps.

▊▊ for holiday gifts on the Internet can be an interesting experience.

INTRODUCING THE STRATEGY

- **Ask students to share with the class what they do when they are reading and bump into a word they do not know. Ask them to also share how well they think their "plans" work.**

Record the responses, including each student's name and the suggested plan, on a transparency or sheet of chart paper. This is excellent diagnostic information that will help you tailor instruction to the specific needs of your class at this time. You may find that many say they just skip the word and go on. Others may say they try to sound it out and then go on. Some may look for smaller words in the new word and try to piece them together. And still others may just make wild guesses without using phonics at all. Notice that none of the "plans" just listed employ any second cross-check to see if the word makes sense.

- **Tell students that today's lesson will introduce a "strategy" with three steps that will help them when they bump into a word they do not know.** Explain that it is a very grown-up strategy that will require them to do more than one thing to determine what the word might be.

- **On the overhead projector, display the transparency with the covered word. Read the sentence to the class and put in an "mmm…" sound when you come to the "unknown word."**

- **Ask students to notice where the covered word is located in the sentence. The first step is to put a finger on the word as a place holder, so that they can easily find it again.** When they are reading in a text book or novel there will not be any sticky notes on the hard words. This step helps transfer the strategy to independent reading situations.

- **Ask students to reread the sentence, adding the "mmm…" sound for the covered word. Then, ask them to guess words that would make sense in the space covered in the sentence.** Record only those suggestions that make sense on the transparency near the covered word.

- **Have the class check word length by looking at the amount of space covered by sticky notes and comparing it to the visual length of the words they have guessed.** Cross out any words that are not the correct length. Add any other words that make sense and are the correct length.

This step helps students who guess "car" when the word is "automobile."

- **Remove the first sticky note and show the beginning letter(s) or onset.** Cross-check to see which of the guessed words makes sense, seems to be the correct length, and begins with the correct letter(s). Cross out the guessed words that do not begin with the uncovered beginning letter(s). If the covered word has not yet appeared as a guess, you may record additional guesses now that the onset is known. Now, look for prefixes, suffixes, and any other known "little" words.

- **Then, uncover all the letters to reveal the covered word.**

- **Reread the sentence and confirm that the word makes sense and matches the letters.** You will be pleased to hear students clap and cheer for themselves when they guess the covered word correctly. **If students don't guess the word you might say, "The word is _____, and it means _____. That was a hard one!"** Continue with the rest of the sentences, making sure that students understand the steps and the order to be used.

- **By the end of five or six sentences you should be able to ask, "What should we do next?" and students should be able to verbalize the strategy.** This is an important step in getting them to use the cross-checking strategy independently.

- **Students need to be praised for using the three-step strategy.** The focus of the lesson initially needs to be on the steps in the strategy, not on the individual words. **Students need to talk about how the three steps allowed them to figure out the word and keep comprehension going as they read.**

- Most students this age will require many teacher-directed, whole-class, or small-group practice sessions with the strategy for it to become part of their reading behavior at the automatic level.

HOW TO USE THIS BOOK

THIS RESOURCE INCLUDES THE FOLLOWING:

★ **12 ready-to-use, full-color transparencies,** including a transparency to introduce the strategy (as shown on the poster). The remaining eleven transparencies are examples involving science, social studies, math, literature, or general themes.

> The transparency showing the three-step strategy makes a great introductory whole-class lesson. In addition, select another transparency that matches a theme or topic currently being studied to provide some practice.

You can use a water-based transparency marker to record student guesses right on the transparency and then erase and reuse the transparency. If a permanent transparency marker is used by mistake, spray some hair spray on a cloth or paper towel and gently rub it over the words to remove them.

★ **24 Guess the Covered Word lessons** (pages 22-59) in five different categories: science, math, social studies, literature, and general themes. These lessons are ready to be made into transparencies on any copier. If you wish, color may be added to the illustrations or border with transparency markers that are permanent or water-based. The five categories were selected to illustrate how this strategy may be used throughout the day in all content areas.

★ **Student Self-Monitoring Checklist** (page 16) By fourth grade most students should be taking responsibility for monitoring their own learning. The "Stay Alert, Watch the Flags!" Checklist can be duplicated and kept in their notebooks to help them track their use of the Guess the Covered Word strategy. They will record date, subject, and word where the strategy was used. There is a place to note the particular "tool" or step used and whether they worked independently or with coaching from the teacher or a classmate.

★ **A Teacher Observation Checklist** (page 17) to help keep track of which students are utilizing the three-step Guess the Covered Word strategy in both teacher-directed and independent-reading situations. Make copies of the chart so it can be used many times. Knowing which students are not using some or any of the steps, either in teacher-directed activities or in independent-reading situations, will help you focus instruction on the areas requiring further teaching and practice. Observing students during a teacher-directed Guess the Covered Word lesson, independent reading, or a conference makes it easy to record mastery of the strategy.

> Use a simple code to record your observations. For example, write an "M" for meaning when the first step is being used effectively, "WL" for word length when the second step is being used, and an "SA" for structural analysis when prefixes, suffixes, known "little" words, and all the letters of the word are considered. Mark an "I" if the observation is being made when the student is working independently and "TD" if the observation is being made during a teacher-directed lesson.

Teachers who carefully observe students who have difficulty in the early stages of reading, regardless of their age, will find students looking to them with a "rescue me" look, guessing wildly when their guesses do not make sense, and looking at the beginning sound and substituting any words that begin with that sound. Each of these responses is an indication of which steps need focused attention. The following list may assist some teachers in this observation and instructional decision-making process:

1. **Ask yourself, "What would make sense in this sentence?"** The student who tries to sound out the word letter by letter, and then blend the sounds back into a word needs this step. Sometimes words are irregular and don't follow any of the phonetic rules.

2. **Check the length of the word. Is it a long word or a short word?** All students can use this cross-checking strategy when meeting new words. It helps most after the "making sense" step. If the word "father" makes sense in the sentence but the word is short, a word like "dad" might work better.

3. **Look at the letters at the beginning of the word that come before the first vowel. Use your finger to cover up the rest of the word while you focus on the beginning sound. Now uncover the rest of the word and check for prefixes, root words, suffixes, and known "little" words. Now check out all the rest of the letters in the word.** If a student asks himself, "What makes sense?" and substitutes that word without looking carefully at the covered word, he needs to focus his attention on the phonics/structural analysis component of the cross-checking strategy. Students may find themselves in situations where their prior knowledge and experience do not help them with "what makes sense," so the phonics step will need to be the first strategy for decoding the word.

The student who only looks at the beginning letter in the word and substitutes any word that starts with that letter, without using context clues for "making sense," also needs this strategy. Checking out *all* the letters in a word keeps the student from guessing a wrong word that may be the same as the right word except for one letter. Examples of these tricky words are words like **bitter**, **batter**, **better**, and **butter**.

★ **The Guess the Covered Word bookmarks** (page 18) can be strategy prompts for students as they learn the strategy, take it to the automatic level, and apply it throughout the day. They are also helpful for at-risk students who need more time and practice. The bookmarks can travel with a student to each reading piece, keeping the strategy steps before his/her eyes for easy rein-

forcement. **Making the strategy function at the automatic level is important, so the bookmark should not be kept as a long-term prompt**.

Fourth Grade Guess the Covered Word offers three different examples of bookmark strategy prompts. Some students will benefit from the bookmark with the mini-illustrations of the racing car from the poster. This strong visual bookmark with the strategy in its simplest form will support visual learners.

A second bookmark provides an example of a sentence with a covered word taken through all the steps. This one will provide support for any student who does not follow all the steps consistently. The example provides the type of support students feel in a teacher-directed lesson.

The third bookmark shows all the steps in creating your own Guess the Covered Word lesson.

★ **A Racing Hall of Fame Recognition chart** (page 19) and **Pit Stop Crew Recognition chart** (page 20) have been included to recognize students who have mastered the strategy steps and use them independently as they read, as well as students who coach others using examples they have created.

Copy the charts and use them to support learning in your classroom by adding the names of the students who qualify. Everyone enjoys positive reinforcement and recognition, especially those who need to work for longer periods of time to master the strategy's application.

★ **A full-color poster** provides the visual stimulus to remind students to apply the strategy. "Stay Alert, Watch the Flags!" uses signal flags and other racing symbols to focus attention on clues that help students to consistently decode more complex, content-area vocabulary.

★ **A mini copy of the poster** (page 21) can be duplicated and given to students for their notebooks. The notebook reminder promotes independent learning at both school and at home for students who are not using the strategy at the automatic level.

★ **High frequency words** for each lesson are listed in the appendix (pages 60-63). The words fall into categories like compound words, words with prefixes or suffixes, often misspelled words, etc.

★ **Content specific words** for each lesson have also been listed in the appendix (pages 60-63). These words expand students' reading, listening, and speaking vocabularies.

★ **A Parent Update** (page 15) is another connection between school and home that keeps family informed. By fourth grade students should be taking the major responsibility for their learning. Make copies of the "Update" and send it home, if it meets the current reading needs of your students.

"PLUS" FACTORS

"Plus" Factor ideas extend the lessons into other instructional activities.

★ **Science Experiment:** Your class or grade level may wish to start a compost pile at school. The cafeteria can supply many of the necessary ingredients. A school garden may have a richer harvest because of your efforts.

★ **Lifetimes:** Provide students with a real understanding about the power of cooperative efforts by taking what we learn from army ants and comparing the information to humans. Begin a class discussion and record the responses to these questions. Are there times when people work together as a large group and accomplish unthinkable tasks? What can we do as a class that we could never accomplish as individuals? Think of other animals or plants where such group cooperation exists. Start an "I wonder" chart in your classroom focusing on the book, *Wonderful Nature, Wonderful You* by Karin Ireland (Dawn Publications, 1996). "I wonder where in the world these army ants live." "I wonder why these ants are so much more dangerous than just plain ants." "I wonder how they got so smart in knowing how to make balls and bridges." To add extra interest and excitement, ask the principal, librarian, or another teacher to provide the first two "I wonders." Have each person record his or her name beside the "I wonder" entry. Periodically, schedule a research trip to the library where students in groups of two or three select one of the "I wonder" statements, find the facts, and give the information to the person who wrote the entry on the chart. Each "I wonder" statement can be selected by only one group. This promotes the use of different resources in the media center and results in several people getting feedback.

★ **Dangerous Weather:** You might start a class notebook and keep track of all major storms. Students could locate areas affected on maps, and summarize data about wind velocity, temperature, and rainfall amounts from news reports. They could also record information relating to property damage. Based on your location, students may have experienced some of these weather conditions personally. In such cases, journal entries provide a rich opportunity to use powerful language in first person writing.

★ **Animals Galore:** Have students select an animal and research information on its habitat and its position on the plentiful to endangered species list. Finding out about what special characteristics the animal has to protect itself might result in facts that will amaze the class.

★ **Life Cycles: Monarch Butterfly:** Nonfiction is a favorite reading genre for fourth graders. They are fascinated with the wonders of nature. A caterpillar changing into a butterfly has always been a showstopper. A small collection of life cycle books could make a research center in the classroom come to life. The assignment could be research done in cooperative learning groups. Ask each group to choose the creature they think makes the most amazing change within its life cycle. Each group can then report their findings to the class.

★ **Life Cycles: Green Snake:** The topic of snakes causes some students to make faces and shriek. Amazing facts about some of these reptiles may result in new interest. Use a KWL chart format, and add a few statements in the K column (see example below).

K	W	L
Clear scales cover some snakes' eyes and allow them to keep their eyes open all the time.		

As a class or in small groups, have students fill in other contributions to the chart.

★ **How 4ᵗʰ Graders Spend Their Leisure Time:** Which of these visual past times—videos, television, movies, computer games, or the Internet—do you predict will be the favorite in your class? Make your predictions and check out the facts by doing a whole class survey. How much leisure time per week do nine-year-olds have? Collect your data. You may have to average the results. Record your results, and analyze the findings. Was there a difference between boys and girls?

★ **Whiz Kid Math Vocabulary:** Start a classroom chart where you record words that are unique to math, along with their definitions. Periodically, use the terms and definitions in a Jeopardy!® format.

★ **Math Solutions:** Explore different ways to make story problems more concrete and easier to solve. Choose a problem where drawing a diagram would help. Write a sentence equation to make sure the correct math processes are being used and in the correct sequence. You could also choose a problem and cross out all the numbers, sentences, or information that should be ignored. Have students suggest other problem-solving strategies they use that are successful.

★ **Survey and Graph:** Complete the trick-or-treat survey and summarize the findings in either paragraph form or by using a Venn diagram. Conducting surveys and graphing combine many skills and instructional opportunities. First, collecting information requires students to formulate questions, and then create a format for recording the data. Comparing and analyzing the data involves organizational skills and more than just literal comprehension. Making predictions also helps develop important reading comprehension skills. Recording, reporting, and evaluating the results of the analysis involve both creative and analytical interpretation.

★ **Television Mysteries:** Students enjoy seeing how unique their fingerprints are. A sponge soaked with red, blue, or green poster paint will allow for the collection of the prints with much easier cleanup than using a stamp pad. You could use a read-aloud from the *Encyclopedia Brown* series to explore the components of a mystery—crime, clues, perpetrator, evidence, detective, and victims.

★ **New Year, New Calendar:** By fourth grade, a student's life becomes crowded with events and activities. Designing a blank monthly calendar that can be copied for students to keep in their notebooks is a good class activity. You might leave a space at the bottom of the calendar to record dates for long-term assignments or special events, like sports or family celebrations. Some students only do homework the night before the assignment is due, and using the calendar can be a way for them to see how to better manage their tasks over a longer period of time.

★ **Newspapers:** Newspapers offer many different reading opportunities. Learning to scan advertisements and compare prices is a good combination reading/math activity. Compiling team scores and player statistics is an easy lead-in to graphing that is also highly motivational. Some "Dear Abby" letters are appropriate for classroom use. After reading several of these letters together, have half the class write their own letters to "Dear Abby," and let the other half of the class respond to their classmates' letters. The topics for the "Dear Abby" letters should be real issues for students at this age level, and the advice should be realistic and appropriate.

★ **You've Got E-Mail:** Pen pals of the past have been replaced by E-mail. Since fourth graders study the state in which they live, it might be interesting to exchange E-mail with another fourth grade class from a school in a different part of their state.

★ **Student Interest Inventory:** Personal interests and preferences are areas where most nine-year-olds consider themselves experts. They have favorite sports, foods, hobbies, television shows, friends, and clothing. This inventory gives students a chance to record, report, and compare their interests to those of others in the class or on their grade level. This activity can produce a high level of participation and positive excitement because the spotlight is on the students and their personal interests.

★ **Stone Fox:** Studying character development is interesting when little Willy takes center stage. Throughout the book, he makes decisions and puts forth effort beyond what is usually found in a nine-year-old. If *Stone Fox* is used as a read-aloud or literature group selection, you can stop at the points in the text where Willy makes a decision and discuss the merits of those decisions. Have students rate how difficult the decisions were to make using a scale from 1-5, with 5 being the most difficult and 1 being the least difficult. They can also rate whether Willy's decisions were wise or not using a scale from 1-5, with 1 being foolish and 5 being wise.

★ **Because Brian Hugged His Mother:** The author, David Rice, uses many words to express the concept "someone felt good." Have students do a "word search" to find these words in the text (e.g., "feeling loved and appreciated," etc.).

★ **Brothers and Sisters:** Generate a class list of the positive and negative aspects of being the oldest, middle, youngest, or only child in a family.

★ **Walt Disney:** Many students think that famous people have always been admired and respected. This may not be true. Walt Disney's original idea to use a small mouse as a recurring character was rejected. He did not give up on his idea, however, and the early criticism was proven wrong when Mickey Mouse® became an international success. His plan for a theme park in California was also not greeted with applause, but his determination did not allow him to be discouraged. Disneyland®, and later Disney World® in Florida, became international vacation spots enjoyed by people of all ages. Ask students to discuss the value of perseverance, and brainstorm ways in which they can encourage each other to reach their goals.

★ **Yeh-Shen: A Cinderella Story from China:** Students can work in small groups and create a compare/contrast chart using a two-circle Venn Diagram format. These student comparisons should include the characters, setting, and plot. This guess the covered word lesson can be a follow-up to a read-aloud of *Yeh-Shen* by the teacher.

★ **The Magic School Bus: At the Water Works:** Create a class version of a *Magic School Bus* book using any topic you are currently studying. The class, in small groups, can share the responsibilities of doing research on the topic, creating the small "notebook pages" that are along the outside edges of the book pages, and doing illustrations. Change "Frizzle" to your name, and you have a one-of-a-kind book to stay in the library and be enjoyed by other classes.

★ **Littlejim's Gift: An Appalachian Christmas Story:** The setting is the Appalachian Mountains at Christmas during World War I, when families were lucky to have the bare necessities. Littlejim works hard to earn money for a tool set he wants, while his little sister desperately wants a doll. When the time comes, which will he buy? Sharing this story with your students may encourage them as a class to adopt a less fortunate family for the holiday.

★ **Timelines…Moments in the Life of John Chapman (alias Johnny Appleseed) :** Here is a chance for your students to explore some key events in the life of a legendary hero. The retelling of the story is written as a flashback. This technique, if explored in a whole class activity, can have a positive influence on students' writing. Begin with the end of a story, and then build the connections in reverse order.

★ **Careers:** Start a class discussion around what activities students are each good at or what skills each student has, then discuss how those can relate to future careers and occupations.

★ **The World of Work:** Survey your class to find the types of jobs held by students' parents. Compile the information and graph the totals. In paragraph form describe the findings. Using the graph found on page 55, compare your class's data to the facts collected by 24 fourth graders who each selected one of their parents' jobs and sorted them into the seven listed categories.

★ **Weather Map:** Model how to play this game with transparency K and the weather cards on page 59. Then, find the largest weather map from the newspaper (e.g., *USA Today*®, etc.) to use as your game board. Cut apart the weather game cards, shuffle them, and place them face down on or near the map. Select two students or two teams of students to play. Students take turns reading the cards. Both students or both teams search the map for the answer(s). The first player or team to locate a correct response earns 10 points. The first player or team to reach 100 points wins! This flexible game can be used with any weather map, and additional questions can be written by the teacher or the class. Have students use a prepared answer key to check their answers.

★ **North Carolina—First in Flight:** A wonderful place to learn about the first flight is at the Wright Brothers National Memorial in Kill Devil Hills. There is a state park nearby at Jockey's Ridge. If you are interested in a wind adventure, you can join many other hang gliders who come especially to enjoy the wind of the Wright Brothers. You can decide to make a visit via your computer at http://www.nps.gov/wrbr. The Dare County Tourist Bureau can also give you more information.

CREATING YOUR OWN GUESS THE COVERED WORD LESSONS

Once you and your class have experienced the power and pleasure of using the Guess the Covered Word strategy, you will want to create some of your own lessons to fit the other content you are studying. The lessons can be used with the whole class or small groups. If students create some examples, they can be made ready by applying sticky notes and used as a student-directed lesson or independent center activity. Later in the year, some students might like to create their own examples and challenge family members to figure out the covered word(s).

Step 1 **Choose a topic for your Guess the Covered Word.**

Example topic: scouting

Step 2 **Make a list of words that are important to the topic.**

campouts	smores
campfires	uniform
merit badges	scoutmaster

Step 3 **Determine the difficulty level.** Covered words are easiest at the end of a sentence, harder in the middle, and hardest at the beginning. Covered words that begin with single consonant onsets are easier to guess than those that begin with blends, digraphs, or prefixes. Words with fewer syllables are easier to guess. Simple sentences are easier than using the strategy in a paragraph where information or clues from earlier sentences may be useful or necessary in determining the covered word.

The following example is a paragraph with covered words at the beginning and end of sentences (mid-level difficulty).

Step 4 **Write sentences with words selected to cover.** Make sure you selected words that begin with a consonant, blend, or digraph. In order for the strategy to be cross-checking, each covered word should be one for which **more than one word** makes sense in the sentence.

Our **scoutmaster** recognizes our accomplishments by awarding merit badges to several troop members. At our recent campout, we enjoyed sharing spooky stories around a campfire, while eating finger-licking good **smores**.

Step 5 **Cover each of the selected words with (1) a sticky note to cover the beginning letter(s) up to the first vowel, and (2) another sticky note to cover the remaining portion of the word.** Remember to make sticky notes only as long as the word, since word length is one of the strategy steps.

Our [   ] recognizes our accomplishments by awarding merit badges to several troop members. At our recent campout, we enjoyed sharing spooky stories around a campfire, while eating finger-licking good [   ].

Step 6 Follow the three steps to make sure your examples work:

1. Ask what words make sense in the sentence.

2. Check the word length.

3. Check the beginning letter(s), prefixes/suffixes, known "little" words, and all the other letters in the word.

Step 7 Challenge your class to "guess the covered words" in your lessons. If the lesson is being led by a student, remind him or her to coach the other students with the strategy steps if they need help.

STUDENT-CREATED GUESS THE COVERED WORD LESSONS

Once students have used the Guess the Covered Word strategy they may want to create some lessons of their own, with some teacher support. A sample planning sheet might be useful for students as they create their own Guess the Covered Word lessons.

A completed plan sheet from a fourth grade student might look like the following:

MAKE YOUR OWN GUESS THE COVERED WORD PLAN SHEET

NAME _John_   DATE _May 12_

My topic is _my best birthday_ .

Some words related to my topic are:

target	refreshments	climbing
practice	presents	
tokens	virtual	
invitations	mountain	

My sentences or paragraph: (Write this on the back of your paper.)

Covered Words	Other Guesses	Beginning Letter(s)
terrific	awesome fun cool	t
virtual	pretend fun scary	v
slipping	falling tumbling	sl
refreshments	food snacks treats	r
frosty	icy delicious large	fr

Having my 9th birthday party at the mall arcade was **terrific**. We wore helmets for some **virtual** mountain climbing. Jeff got up the highest without **slipping**. For **refreshments** we each had a roll of tokens to use in all the snack machines. We had plenty of chips, popcorn, candy, and **frosty** drinks.

Parent Update

_____
Date

Dear Family,

We have been learning lots of ways to become better readers. We meet challenging new words in social studies and science, like **scrumptious** and **consume**. Guess the Covered word is a three-step strategy that requires us to use comprehension, word length, phonics, and word analysis skills. I'd like to use this example to show you how it works.

> What would a million marching army ants call a **delectable** dinner? Bunches of insects, **spiders,** or other small animals would do. Or they might **consume** an animal as large as a horse or a tiger if it was unable to retreat. Wow! That's really awesome!

Steps for the Guess the Covered Word Strategy

If there is a word in a sentence you don't know:

1. Cover the word with your finger, (for the example above, use the word delectable) then continue reading the rest of the sentence.
2. Ask yourself, "What would make sense?" Record some of the possibilities.
3. Check out the word length. Compare the space the word takes up in the sentence to the words you thought were possibilities.
4. Look at the beginning letter(s) up to the first vowel (a, e, i, o, u) and compare it to the list of possibilities.
5. Uncover the whole word and check for prefixes, root words, suffixes, or known "little" words.
6. After checking all the letters and clues, reread the sentence with the new word, and double-check to make sure it makes sense in the sentence.

I know you want me to become a good reader so I can learn many new things. Thanks for taking the time to let me show you what we are learning.

Love,

_____

 # Stay Alert, Watch the Flags!
Student Self-Monitoring Checklist

Date	Subject/Word	What makes sense?	Length of word	Letter(s)/ sounds	By myself	Got help
3/6	math/predictions	estimations	✓	pr	✓	

Teacher Observation Chart

Code Key

M = Makes sense   **I** = Independent
WL = Checks word length   **TD** = Teacher Directed
SA = Structural Analysis (first letter(s), prefixes,
     suffixes, known "little" words, all the other letters
     in the word)
✓ = Uses all three steps in order consistently

Name	Date / Code	Date / Code	Comments
Jake	9/9 TD ✓	10/15 I ✓	Sentences automatic
Michael	9/9 TD SA	10/15 TD ✓	OK Check again
Juliana	9/9 TD M	10/15 TD M WL	Focus on what makes sense

Name	Date / Code	Date / Code	Date / Code	Comments

Bookmarks

FOLLOW THE STEPS TO GUESS THE COVERED WORD

Doing the **bibliography** for my report was the most difficult part of my assignment.

Where is the word? Cover the word to keep your place.

Doing the ▮▮▮▮▮ for my report was the most difficult part of my assignment.

What makes sense?
research
bibliography
draft

Check word length.

Doing the ▮▮▮▮▮ for my report was the most difficult part of my assignment.

Check the beginning sound. Check for parts you know.
b
bib
bibliography

Did you guess the covered word?

© Carson-Dellosa

Create Your Own Guess the Covered Word

1. Select a topic of interest where you know many words.

2. Make a list of words and choose one that begins with a consonant, blend, or digraph.

3. Decide if the word will be at the beginning, middle, or end of the sentence.

4. Write the sentence and make sure that more than one word will make sense as the covered word.

5. Cover the word with sticky notes. Put one note over the beginning sound(s). Put another sticky note over the rest of the word.

6. Challenge your class-mates with your covered word lesson.

© Carson-Dellosa

Is there a word you don't know?

START

Where is the word?

THINK
What makes sense?

LOOK
How long is the word?

LOOK & LISTEN

- What is the beginning sound(s)? Are there any prefixes or suffixes? Are there any known "little" words? Look at all the other letters.

© Carson-Dellosa

18

Racing Hall of Fame
Recognition Chart

These students have mastered all the steps in the Guess the Covered Word strategy. They use the strategy independently as they read. They also support the learning of others by coaching their classmates in using the strategy.

_____   _____   _____

_____   _____   _____

_____   _____   _____

_____   _____   _____

_____   _____   _____

_____   _____   _____

_____   _____   _____

_____   _____   _____

_____   _____   _____

Pit Stop Crew
Recognition Chart

Students listed here have been Guess the Covered Word coaches with classmates, and have created their own examples.

_____ _____ _____

_____ _____ _____

_____ _____ _____

_____ _____ _____

_____ _____ _____

_____ _____ _____

_____ _____ _____

_____ _____ _____

STAY ALERT! WATCH THE FLAGS!

1 START
Where is the word?
Beginning–Middle–End

2 THINK
What makes sense?

3 LOOK
How long is the word?

4 LISTEN
How does the word begin?
Are there any word parts you know?
Check all the letters.

What should you do when you bump into an unknown word?

FINISH LINE

Cross the finish line with the Guess the Covered Word strategy!

Science Experiment

Ashley and Miguel were excited about the class science **project.** Teams of students each buried an apple in the ground and observed it **decompose** over time. One team noticed that the apple decomposed more **readily** in clay soil than in sandy soil. Other students found the warm, **moist** conditions made the apple decay more quickly. All the young scientists were glad they had magnifying lenses to help them better **view** small changes. The experiment encouraged students to start **compost** heaps at home.

22

Lifetimes

Lifetimes by David L. Rice (Dawn Publications, 1997)

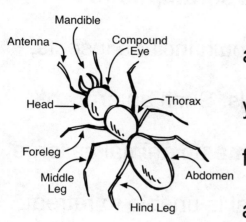

Did you know that the **lifetime** of an army ant is approximately three years long? Army ants are known for their amazing **collective** accomplishments.

They look like soldiers when they march from place to place, sometimes in a group as big as a **million.** Wow! That is a lot of ants to see coming to your **location.**

They are **determined** and unstoppable in what they can accomplish. When they come to a river, some of them create a **bridge** with their bodies and the rest of the ants walk across. If the river is too wide to form a bridge, they form "antballs" and **float** across.

Lifetimes (page 2)

What would this army call a **scrumptious**

dinner? Their menu of choice would include insects,

spiders, and other small animals. Such an army of

ants has been known to **consume** an animal as large

as a horse or a tiger if the animal is unable to retreat.

People who live in areas with army ants

may evacuate their homes for a day or two

when the ants **descend** upon their area.

When the homeowners return, their houses

are completely free of cockroaches and

rodents. I think I'd rather call pest control—

how about you?

Dangerous Weather

The whole class heard the **forecaster** predict a hurricane. Some students made a list of how their families prepared by purchasing extra **batteries** and supplies. Our teacher thought **water** and canned food were the most important items to have on hand in a possible emergency. We all listened to the weather updates **continuously.** The predictions were for heavy rains with up to 10 inches of rainfall leading to rivers **cresting** by morning. We knew that winds exceeding 100 miles per hour could **spawn** tornadoes and cause millions of dollars in damages.

25

Dangerous Weather (page 2)

Major evacuations would be necessary to **prevent** loss of life and keep severe injuries to a minimum. The hurricane's course indicated it should make landfall near **Wilmington.** We understood that the best way to be safe in such weather is to be **knowledgeable** about current conditions and to be prepared.

Animals Galore

The class was doing a report on local **wildlife** that required using multiple sources of information to learn about each animal's **habitat**. Does the animal primarily live on land or in water, or in a field, a tree, or a **desert**? Is the animal

endangered or **plentiful**? How does the animal **coexist** with people—are they mutually helpful or antagonistic?

Many students included how animals protect themselves by playing dead and using quills or **camouflage**. Students used books, videos, and the Internet to research food chains and unique **characteristics** like long necks or pouches.

How 4ᵗʰ Graders Spend Their Leisure Time

How much **leisure** time do the fourth graders you know have and how do they spend it? Some like to work **solo** on hobbies like stamp collecting. Others **prefer** group activities like sports. Many **select** active choices like jogging or more passive activities like reading or computers. Some are involved in clubs or **scouts.**

Leisure Time (page 2)

How Fourth Graders Spend Their Time

Read Books	Ride Bike	Work on Computer	Scouting	Sports	Other

Whiz Kid Math Vocabulary

We usually think about **numbers** when we talk about math. But there are many words that are only used in **mathematics.** Words like remainder and **quotient** belong to the division operation.

Learning about **fractions** invites lots of words to cross your path. Terms like **denominator,** lowest terms, and mixed numbers are like a new language. Geometry introduces shape words like triangle, **hexagon,** and sphere.

Wow! Math is full of new, **challenging** vocabulary.

Math Solutions

Marcos felt like solving math problems was impossible and **frustrating.** His teacher and classmates **supported** him with encouragement and new strategies to use. One classmate shared how drawing a **diagram** can help you to understand the information in a word problem. Travis told how he uses a computer **spreadsheet** to sort out important facts from irrelevant facts.

Math Solutions (page 2)

Shelly focuses her attention on **sequencing** the steps and writing equations to solve a complex problem.

After a little help from his classmates, Marcos was feeling better and contributed how important it is to check the answer and see if a decimal point or a **percent** sign is required.

Survey and Graph

It all originated with a student reading an article in the newspaper about what kinds of **treats** nine-year olds like best in their trick-or-treat bags. The **results** came up with surprising outcomes. The choices of this generation's adults who will purchase the candy given out, did not match with the **preferences** of the consumers—trick-or-treaters.

Our fourth grade class decided to select 12 treats and survey fourth graders and their parents and see if their "tastes" are **compatible**. We decided to report the results in two different **formats**. Some of us will **disseminate** our findings in paragraph form while others will do graphs or Venn diagrams.

Survey and Graph (page 2)

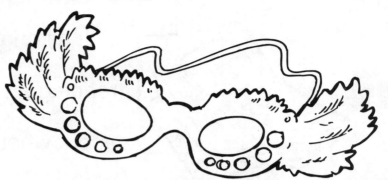

Our first assignment was to get **consensus** from everyone for which twelve treats would appear on the survey. The survey **contains** both candy names and illustrations so everyone has a good idea of what the treats look like. The survey also has a place to indicate whether the **data** is coming from a fourth grader or a parent. It includes a box for each treat where the individual **records** a ranking from 1-12 for that treat. Number 1 is the favorite treat from the list and number 12 ranks the treat as the least **preferred**. Each number from 1-12 can only be used once.

Trick-or-Treat Survey

Think about going trick-or-treating. What things would you be happy to find in your treat bag at the end of your adventure? Look at each of the 12 treats below and put a 1 in the box by the treat which would be your favorite. Then, put a 12 in the box by the treat which you would least like. Now go back and label your next favorite 2, and the next 3, and so on. If you are a parent buying treats place a 1 beside the treat you will most likely purchase. Place a 12 beside the treat you would be least likely to buy and so on.

Check a box to identify who you are.

[ ] parent   [ ] 4th grader

| Hershey's Kisses [ ] | Tootsie Roll® [ ] | Gummy Fruit [ ] | Candy Corn [ ] |

| Reese's Pieces® [ ] | M & M's® [ ] | Sweet Tarts® [ ] | Hershey's Bar [ ] |

| Blow Pop® [ ] | Snickers® [ ] | LifeSavers® [ ] | Taffy [ ] |

35

Television Mysteries

Juan loves to watch **mysteries** on television. There is something about gathering the **clues** or evidence in a case that intrigues him. Stepping into the detective's shoes allows him to figure out who's the **perpetrator**. In order to get a **conviction**, he must figure out the 3 M's or M.O.M. The **motive** refers to the "reason for the crime." The **means** or opportunity refers to the ability to commit the crime. The **method** refers to the weapon used like a gun or a knife.

Television Mysteries (page 2)

Detectives investigate and gather evidence from the clues at the crime scene. Fingerprints, footprints, skid marks, and even tire tracks help establish who the **criminal** might be. Telephone records, lie detector tests, alibis, and eyewitness **testimony** help prove the guilt or innocence of a defendant.

New Year, New Calendar

José wanted to create a **calendar** for nine- and ten-year olds for the new year. He saw a **selection** at the bookstore but found none that he liked. He imagined a design with all the **features** that students would like. Bill was eager to provide the **photographs** for the cover and inside. The whole class **volunteered** to add a thought and activity for each day. Michael explored several computer programs that allowed us to personalize the calendar with **graphics** to suit personal taste. Everyone in the class was pleased with their **cooperative** effort.

You've Got E-mail

Max's class in San Francisco, California was **participating** in an E-mail project with a class in Dallas, Texas. Luis and Lisa shared facts about famous **bridges** that surround San Francisco, like the Golden Gate Bridge. They shared recipes for ethnic **favorites** like Chinese stir-fry, Thai noodles, fajitas, and Japanese shrimp tempura. Hank loved seeing the pictures of these **finger-licking** new cultural foods.

Meanwhile, Hank and his classmates described a Texas barbeque with steaks and ribs **smothered** in delicious sauces. Descriptions of rounding up a herd of cattle for branding **fascinated** their West Coast audience. Pictures of **feats** from a local rodeo and the Alamo instantaneously speed across the miles and have Max, Luis, and Lisa watching wide-eyed in amazement. The **telecommunication** project was enjoyed by all who were involved.

Name:_____ Date:_____

Student Inventory

Some of my hobbies are _____

_____.

Things I like to collect are _____

_____.

My favorite sport is _____

_____.

I like to read books about _____

_____.

Some of my favorite Web sites are _____

_____.

A school adult I respect is _____

because _____

_____.

My favorite part of the school day is _____.

If I had $50 to spend, the first thing I would buy is

_____.

If I could teach another student something, it would

be _____

_____.

The neatest thing I ever learned was _____

_____.

The one thing I would like to learn most this year is

_____.

I am really good at _____

_____.

41

Sample Class Inventory

Zack and Antonio like to **collect** key chains.

The sport most of us in this class chose as their favorite was **soccer**.

Kaleb and Ruth would buy **Nintendo**® games with $50.

Vanessa most admires her **teacher** because this person always smiles and listens to her.

Many of the **favorite** Web sites were ones that had games.

Recess was not the favorite part of the school day, but computer class was!

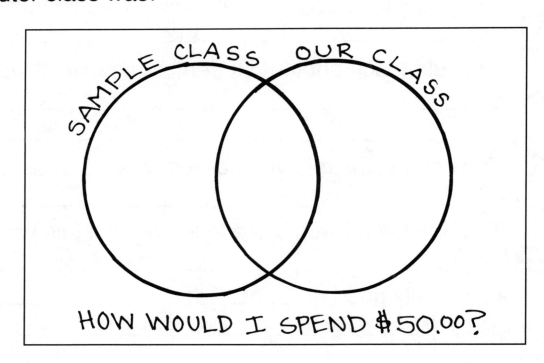

HOW WOULD I SPEND $50.00?

Brothers and Sisters

Are you the youngest, middle, oldest, or only child in your family?

What special **responsibilities** and privileges does the oldest child have?

Does the oldest child ever have to clean up after or **babysit** the younger ones?

Does the oldest get to pick first when there is a **choice**, and does she have a later bedtime?

Does the middle child sometimes get hand-me-down **clothes** or almost-new toys?

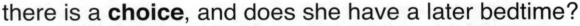

As the youngest, does a child get **special** help and attention from everyone?

What makes being an only child **fantastic**?

Words, Words, Compound Words

Sometimes we "piggyback" or combine two words to make one word we call a **compound** word.

Lots of words piggyback with "some" to make more difficult **vocabulary**.

The five letter word "where" piggybacks with another word to make **somewhere.**

Piggyback by adding to the beginning of "ball" and make **basketball.**

Piggyback by adding to the beginning of "side" and make "**beside.**"

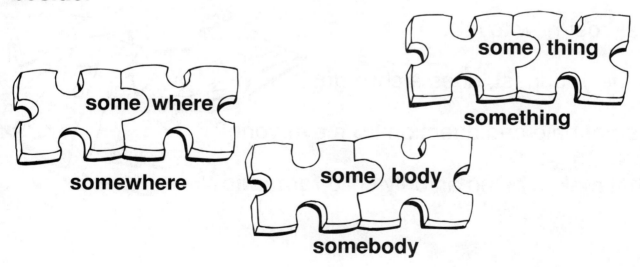

somewhere

some thing

something

some body

somebody

44

Stone Fox

Stone Fox by John Reynolds Gardiner (HarperTrophy, 1980)

Little Willy, his dog Searchlight, and Willy's grandpa lived **contentedly** on their potato farm. Willy was **clueless** about what to do when Grandpa suddenly refused to get out of bed or speak. Willy and Searchlight worked **diligently** to bring in the potato crop. His grandpa's strange behavior was explained when Willy learned about the $500 owed in back taxes and the upcoming **repossession** of the farm.

A solution to the **dilemma** was possible when Willy learned of the dogsled race where the winning prize was $500.

45

Stone Fox (page 2)

Willy realized that his real **rival** would be a Native American named Stone Fox who managed to win every race he ever entered.

Little Willy took the risk and **gambled** all the cash the family had for the entry fee. For most of the race, Willy was in the lead, and he was feeling **confident**. As they approached town and the finish line, something unexpected and **catastrophic** occurred. This story's powerful **conclusion** makes readers and listeners of any age sniffle.

Because Brian Hugged His Mother

Because Brian Hugged His Mother by David L. Rice (Dawn Publications, 1999)

One morning a young lad named Brian started his day by giving his mother a big **squeeze**. This hug gets passed on throughout the story as each character does something **positive** for the next one.

Brian's mom felt loved and appreciated so she fixed **waffles** for breakfast. Brian's sister Joanna felt so good she helped her **teacher**.

This amusing, positive cumulative tale reminds us of the power of positive behaviors and **deeds**.

Yeh-Shen: A Chinese Cinderella Tale

Yeh-Shen: A Cinderella Story from China by Ai-Ling Louie (Puffin Books, 1974)

Cinderella exists in many **cultures**, but this Chinese version may be the original tale. Yeh-Shen was an orphan growing up in the home of her **stepmother**. Her stepsister was jealous of her and often showed her **displeasure** by making Yeh-Shen do all the unpleasant chores.

Her stepmother learned about the fish with the golden eyes which was Yeh-Shen's special **companion**. When the fish was caught and cooked, Yeh-Shen **collapsed**. She learned that the bones of her fish were filled with **magical** influence.

Yeh-Shen: A Chinese Cinderella Tale (page 2)

The fish's bones provided her with food when she was **famished**. When she had nothing to wear to the **festival,** the bones provided beautiful sandals and attire. Yeh-Shen left the festival in a hurry and lost her golden sandal, which was **gorgeous**. In the traditional manner, the king searches the land for its owner and is **betrothed** to Yeh-Shen.

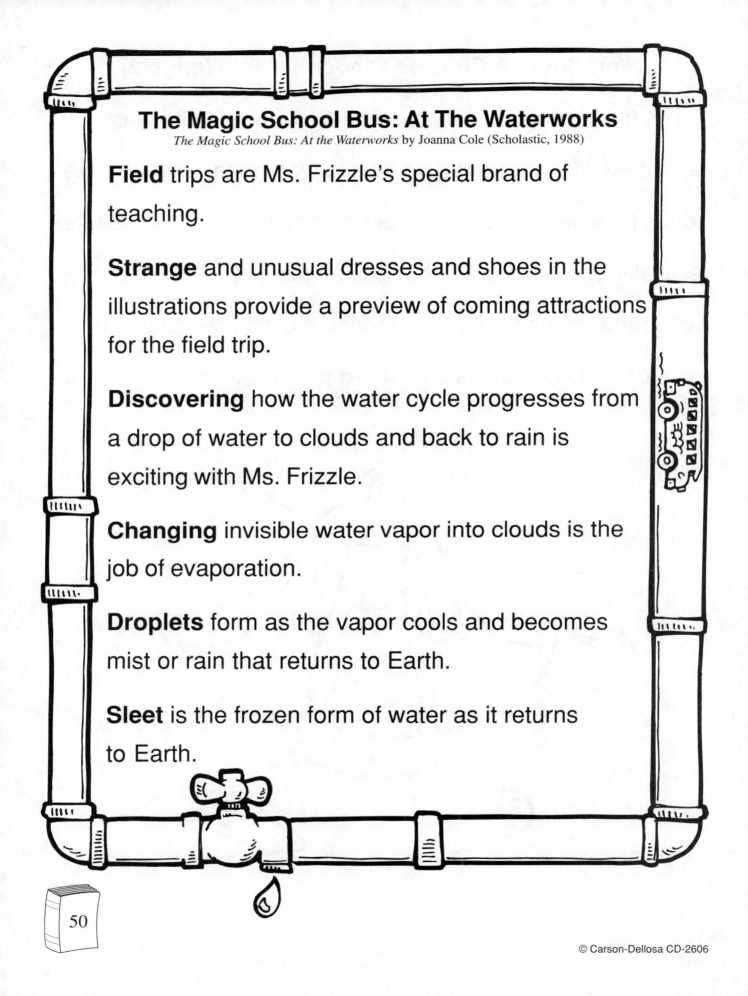

The Magic School Bus: At The Waterworks

The Magic School Bus: At the Waterworks by Joanna Cole (Scholastic, 1988)

Field trips are Ms. Frizzle's special brand of teaching.

Strange and unusual dresses and shoes in the illustrations provide a preview of coming attractions for the field trip.

Discovering how the water cycle progresses from a drop of water to clouds and back to rain is exciting with Ms. Frizzle.

Changing invisible water vapor into clouds is the job of evaporation.

Droplets form as the vapor cools and becomes mist or rain that returns to Earth.

Sleet is the frozen form of water as it returns to Earth.

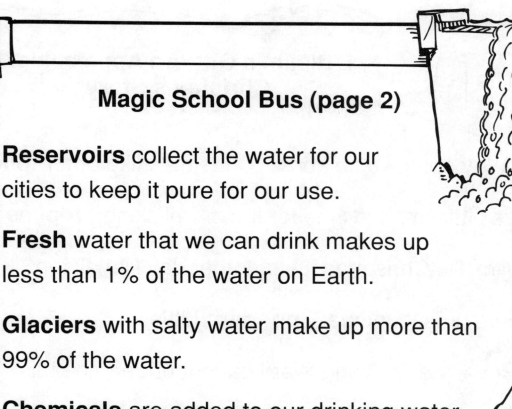

Magic School Bus (page 2)

Reservoirs collect the water for our cities to keep it pure for our use.

Fresh water that we can drink makes up less than 1% of the water on Earth.

Glaciers with salty water make up more than 99% of the water.

Chemicals are added to our drinking water to keep us free from disease, germs, and to prevent cavities.

51

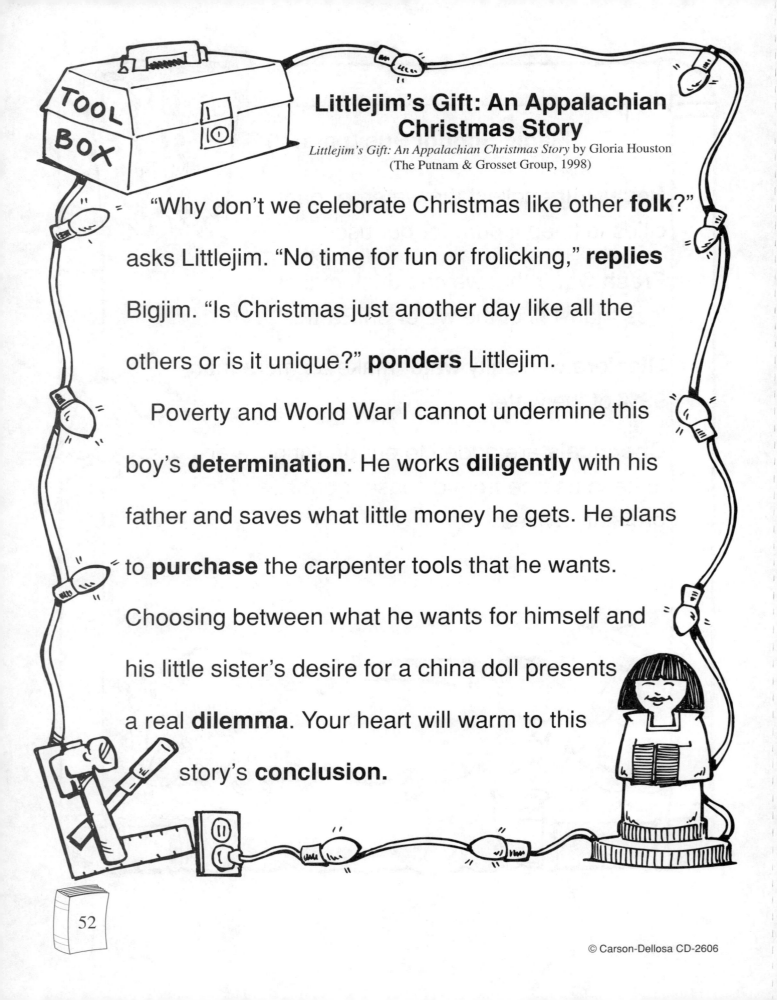

Littlejim's Gift: An Appalachian Christmas Story

Littlejim's Gift: An Appalachian Christmas Story by Gloria Houston
(The Putnam & Grosset Group, 1998)

"Why don't we celebrate Christmas like other **folk**?" asks Littlejim. "No time for fun or frolicking," **replies** Bigjim. "Is Christmas just another day like all the others or is it unique?" **ponders** Littlejim.

Poverty and World War I cannot undermine this boy's **determination**. He works **diligently** with his father and saves what little money he gets. He plans to **purchase** the carpenter tools that he wants. Choosing between what he wants for himself and his little sister's desire for a china doll presents a real **dilemma**. Your heart will warm to this story's **conclusion.**

52

Careers

When Kevin was younger he **considered** talking about careers at school boring. Now the whole class thinks that career **conversations** are fascinating. Shelly enjoys drawing so she wants to be a **designer** or illustrator. Josh shows real talent in writing so he might be a **reporter**. Bill can play the guitar and piano by ear so he might become a professional **musician**. Alex is gifted in math and loves to work with numbers and charts so he might be a **banker** or an accountant. As more of us shared, it was obvious that in the future there would be a **cartoonist**, inventor, comedian, teacher, and a computer programmer from our group.

The World of Work

It **requires** a lot of people to keep our world operating. There are many different kinds of **careers**. The important thing about jobs and occupations is that they take care of something that is **vital** or essential. Individuals are paid wages or salaries for the jobs they **perform**. They take the money they earn and purchase other **services,** like legal or medical help, or goods like a car or groceries. This exchange of money, goods, and services makes our towns, cities, states, and country have a **strong** economy. Think about the **contributions** your parents make to the economy. Every job or career that is honest and needed is **valuable** to our world.

54

Job Survey

Compile information about the job or career held by a parent or adult you know. Use the categories on this graph to report the combined results of the class. Add another group if necessary.

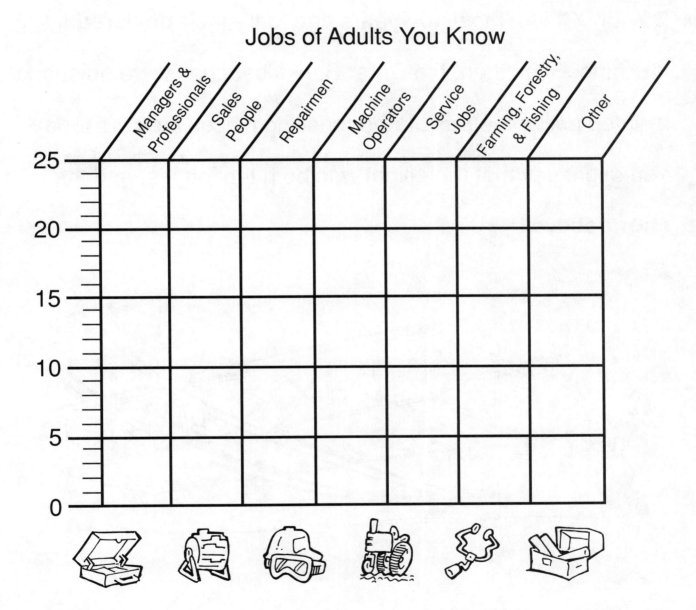

Jobs of Adults You Know

55

North Carolina: First in Flight

Let's take a **flight** back in time. A lot has changed since Orville and Wilbur Wright were **strolling** on the sand at Kill Devil Hills, North Carolina. The famous brothers came from Dayton, Ohio almost 100 years ago to try their **powered** flying machine. Back then, the Outer Banks beaches were quiet and isolated unlike the **populated**, bustling places they are today. You might say that their flight was both the longest and the **shortest** ever.

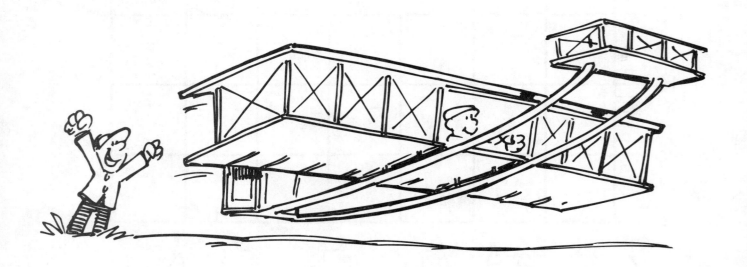

56

Their new flying machine flew just 120 feet and **remained** in the air only 12 seconds. It earned the Wright Brothers a **prominent** place in our history books. A crewman from a nearby lifesaving station snapped a photograph to record the **historic** moment. The **spotlight** shows three aircraft from then to now.

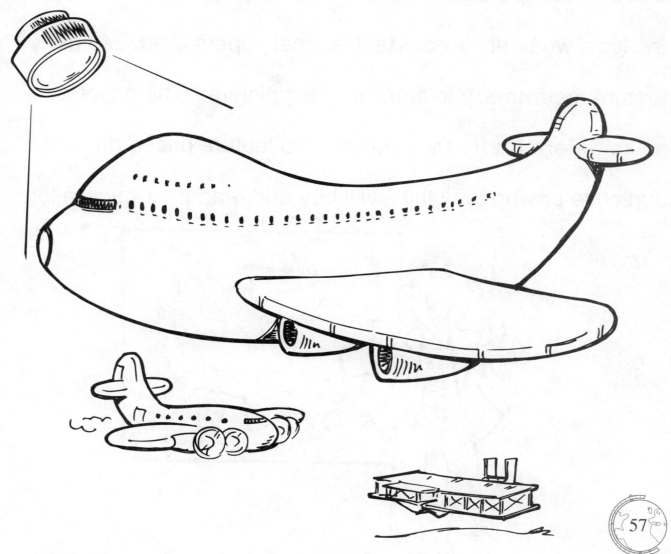

57

Reading a Weather Map

"Everybody **complains** about the weather but no one does anything about it." This is an expression you may have heard elderly family members like **grandparents** say. Newspapers **report** local, regional, national, and worldwide weather especially when violent storms or weather conditions occur. Daily newspapers give a great deal of space to and focus on the local weather **forecasts**. National papers like USA Today® feature a **summary** to show the "big picture." The editors make **determinations** about what to feature based on their audience or who they think will buy and read their publication.

58

Cut these cards apart and place them on the weather map to play the

WEATHER GAME

This is the coolest place that is farthest North.

It is sunny.

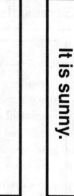

It is snowing.

This is the warmest place that is farthest South.

There is a full moon.

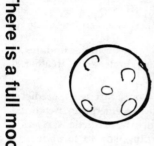

The water is most likely warm.

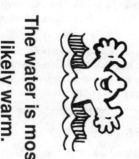

The temperature is below 70° F.

It is raining.

It is the coolest place.

Cooler air is coming in.

It is the warmest city.

The temperature is above 90° F.

59

Appendix

Page 22—Science Experiment

project .... experiment, activity
decompose .... rot, decay
readily .... completely, quickly
moist .... wet, damp
view .... see, observe
compost .... scrap, garbage

- High-frequency words: **were, about, one, quickly, excited**
- Content specific words: **project, observed, decompose, clay soil, sandy soil, warm, moist conditions, scientists, magnifying lenses, experiment, view, compost heaps**

Pages 23-24—Lifetimes

lifetime .... life span
collective .... incredible, group
million .... thousand, billion
location .... environment, community
determined .... stubborn, strong
bridge .... bridge
float .... swim, roll
scrumptious .... delicious, tasty
spiders .... mice, bugs
consume .... eat, devour
descend .... come, march
rodents .... critters, rats

- High-frequency words: **lifetime, their, they, too, sometimes, coming, unstoppable, across**
- Content specific words: **army ants, amazing, collective accomplishments, location, approximately, determined, unstoppable, bridge, antballs, scrumptious, menu of choice, consume, evacuate, descend, cockroaches, rodents, pest control**

Pages 25-26—Dangerous Weather

forecaster .... meteorologist, man, reports
batteries .... food, groceries
water .... food, matches
continuously .... constantly, regularly
cresting .... flooding, overflowing
spawn .... brew, spin off
prevent .... eliminate, stop
Wilmington .... Charleston, Hilton Head
knowledgeable .... wise, knowing, smart

- High-frequency words: **whole, updates, rainfall, exceeding, understood, weather, prepared**
- Content specific words: **forecaster, predict a hurricane, batteries, emergency, weather updates, continuously, predictions, rivers cresting, exceeding, spawn tornadoes, damages, major evacuations, make landfall, knowledgeable**

Page 27—Animals Galore

wildlife .... animals, creatures
habitat .... home, environment
desert .... forest, jungle
plentiful .... abundant, common
coexist .... live, deal
camouflage .... coloring, hiding
characteristics .... features, traits

- High-frequency words: **doing, wildlife, using, coexist, people**
- Content specific words: **local wildlife, animal's habitat, endangered, plentiful, coexist, antagonistic, camouflage, Internet, research, food chains, unique, pouches, characteristics**

Page 28—How 4th Graders Spend Their Leisure Time

leisure .... extra, fun
solo .... alone
prefer .... like, choose
select .... choose, like
scouts .... sports

- High-frequency words: **know, jogging**
- Content specific words: **leisure, solo, hobbies, prefer, select, active choices, passive activities**

Page 30—Whiz Kid Math Vocabulary

numbers .... figures, transactions
mathematics .... math, arithmetic
quotient .... divisor, dividend
fractions .... decimals, percentages
denominator .... numerator, reduce
hexagon .... octagon, pentagon
challenging .... hard, interesting, difficult

- High-frequency words: **usually, invites, lowest, geometry, introduces, challenging**
- Content specific words: **mathematics, remainder, quotient, division operation, fractions, denominator, triangle, hexagon, sphere, lowest terms**

Pages 31-32—Math Solutions

frustrating .... hard, difficult
supported .... helped, cheered
diagram .... picture, chart
spreadsheet ...... program, tools
sequencing .... ordering, listing
percent .... dollars, cent

- High-frequency words: **classmates, understand, information, computer, focuses, attention**
- Content specific words: **impossible, frustrating, supported, strategies, encouragement, diagram, spreadsheet, irrelevant facts, sequencing the steps, solve a complex problem, writing equations, decimal point, percent sign**

Pages 33-34—Survey and Graph

treats .... candy, goodies

results .... answers, data, information

preferences ...... choices, selections

compatible .... identical, alike, similar

formats .... ways, forms

disseminate ...... share, report, summarize

consensus .... agreement, approval

contains .... has, involves, includes

data .... choices, information

records .... indicates, shows

preferred .... enjoyed, liked

- High-frequency words: **newspaper, results, generation's, decided, survey, their, different, formats, assignment, everyone, whether**

- Content specific words: **originated, article, results, surprising outcomes, purchase, this generation's adults, preferences, consumers, select, compatible, disseminate, consensus, indicate, ranking, preferred**

Pages 36-37—Television Mysteries

mysteries .... dramas, sitcoms

clues .... facts, details

perpetrator ...... criminal, crook

conviction .... arrest

motive .... motive

means .... means

method .... method

detectives .... cops, sleuths

criminal .... outlaw, crook

testimony .... report, retelling

- High-frequency words: **television, something, stepping, who's**

- Content specific words: **mysteries, clues, evidence, intrigues, detective, perpetrator, conviction, motive, method, means, investigate, fingerprints, footprints, skid marks, tire tracks, criminal, lie detector tests, alibis, eyewitness testimony, guilt, innocence, defendant**

Page 38—New Year, New Calendar

calendar .... calendar, planner

selection .... variety, colllection

features .... things, elements

photographs .... photos, illustrations

volunteered ...... agreed, promised

graphics .... pictures, photos

cooperative ...... joint, group

- High-frequency words: **bookstore, imagined, provide, inside, explored, several, everyone**

- Content specific words: **calendar, selection, features, photographs, volunteered, computer programs, personalize, graphics, personal taste, cooperative effort**

Pages 39-40—You've Got E-Mail

participating .... involved, engaged

bridges .... parks, statues

favorites .... foods, dishes

finger-licking .... delicious, fantastic

smothered .... covered, dripping

fascinated .... amazed, dazzled

feats .... branding, events

telecommunication E-mail, technology

- High-frequency words: **famous, surround, finger-licking, meanwhile, classmates, described, smothered, delicious, fascinated, instantaneously, wide-eyed, amazement**

- Content specific words: **participating, E-mail, Golden Gate Bridge, recipes for ethnic favorites, Chinese stir-fry, Thai noodles, fajitas, Japanese shrimp tempura, rounding up a herd of cattle, rodeo, Alamo, telecommunication project**

Page 42—Sample Class Inventory

collect .... find, keep

soccer .... baseball, football

Nintendo® .... computer, Pokémon™

teacher .... mother, father

favorite .... best, chosen

recess .... music, art

- High-frequency words: **favorite, buy**

- Content specific words: **collect, soccer, Nintendo®, admires, Web sites, recess**

Pages 43—Brothers and Sisters

responsibilities .... jobs, duties

babysit .... watch

choice .... selection

clothes .... shirts, pants, jackets

special .... more, needed, extra

fantastic .... great, good, wonderful

- High-frequency words: **are, your, what, have, first, when, there, sometimes, almost, new**

- Content specific words: **babysit, responsibilities**

Page 44—Words, Words, Compound Words

compound .... new, different

vocabulary .... words

somewhere .... something, sometimes

basketball .... football, baseball

beside .... inside, outside

- High-frequency words: **words, two, to, one, with, where, another, by**

- Content specific words: **compound, vocabulary**

Pages 45-46—Stone Fox

contentedly .... happily, together

clueless .... blank, unsure

diligently .... hard, continuously

repossession .... takeover, selling

dilemma .... problem, situation

rival .... competition, challenger

gambled .... risked, used, spent

confident .... sure, positive

catastrophic .... disastrous, terrible

conclusion .... end, climax

- High-frequency words: **searchlight, grandpa, their, clueless, suddenly, behavior, explained, owed, upcoming, realized, managed, entered, approached, something, powerful**

Appendix

- Content specific words: **contentedly, clueless, refused, diligently, explained, back taxes, repossession of the farm, solution to the dilemma, rival, gambled, entry fee, confident, unexpected, catastrophic, conclusion**

Page 47—Because Brian Hugged His Mother

squeeze	hug, kiss
positive	nice, wonderful
waffles	pancakes, eggs
teacher	sister, friend
deeds	actions, feelings

- High-frequency words: **started, giving, passed, throughout, something, amusing**
- Content specific words: **squeeze, character, positive, appreciated, cumulative tale, power of positive behaviors and deeds**

Pages 48-49—Yeh-Shen: Chinese Cinderella

cultures	countries, places
stepmother	father, parents
displeasure	unhappiness, jealousy
companion	friend, pet
collapsed	cried, fainted
magical	special, unique
famished	hungry, starving
festival	celebration, party
gorgeous	beautiful, lovely
betrothed	married, engaged

- High-frequency words: **exists, version, learned, caught, provided, searches**
- Content specific words: **cultures, orphan, Chinese, jealous, stepmother, displeasure, unpleasant chores, special companion, collapsed, magical influence, famished, festival, sandals, attire, gorgeous, traditional manner, betrothed**

Pages 50-51—The Magic Schoolbus: At the Waterworks

field	school, class
strange	unique, weird
discovering	exploring, seeing
changing	altering
droplets	drops, clouds
sleet	snow, ice
reservoirs	rivers, lakes
fresh	clean, clear
glaciers	oceans, seas
chemicals	chlorine, flouride

- High-frequency words: **special, unusual, illustrations, preview, rain, surrounds, through, invisible, returns, cities, salty**
- Content specific words: **field trips, preview, coming attractions, water cycle, evaporation, invisible water vapor, sleet, reservoirs, glaciers, chemicals, cavities**

Page 52—Littlejim's Gift: An Appalachian Christmas Story

folk	people, families
replies	says, explains
ponders	asks, wonders
determination	courage, guts
diligently	hard, continuously
purchase	buy, get
dilemma	problem
conclusion	ending, climax

- High-frequency words: **celebrate, unique, ponders, purchase, choosing, between, himself**
- Content specific words: **frolicking, replies, ponders, poverty, undermine, diligently, determination, carpenter tools, dilemma, conclusion**

Page 53—Careers

considered	thought, believed
conversations	discussions, talks
designer	artist, cartoonist
reporter	writer, journalist
musician	pianist, guitarist
banker	teller, auditor
cartoonist	engineer, preacher, nurse

- High-frequency words: **younger, considered, fascinating, become, obvious**
- Content specific words: **careers, career conversations, designer, illustrator, reporter, professional musician, banker, accountant, cartoonist, inventor, comedian, teacher, computer programmer**

Page 54—World of Work

requires	takes, involves
careers	jobs, professions
vital	necessary, important
perform	do, have
services	things, stuff
strong	healthy, fantastic
contributions	additions, help
valuable	useful, important

- High-frequency words: **requires, people, operating, something, individuals, purchase**
- Content specific words: **careers, jobs, occupations, vital, essential, wages, salaries, services, goods, exchange of money, strong, economy, valuable, contributions**

Pages 56-57—North Carolina: First in Flight

flight	trip, journey
strolling	walking, standing
powered	amazing
populated	busy, crowded
shortest	quickest, fastest
remained	stayed, hovered
prominent	permanent, special
historic	special, unique
spotlight	floodlight, light

- High-frequency words: **changed, strolling, famous, quiet, unlike**
- Content specific words: **flight, strolling, Kill Devil Hills, powered flying machine, Outer Banks, isolated, populated, bustling, places, prominent place, historic moment**

Page 58—Reading a Weather Map

complains .... gripes, talks
grandparents ..... parents,
grandmothers
report .... share, tell
forecasts .... reports, predictions
summary .... maps, chart
determinations .. decisions, selections

- High-frequency words: **everybody, about, anything, worldwide, complains, determinations**
- Content specific words: **weather, regional, national, worldwide, conditions, forecasts, show the big picture**

Pages A-B—Life Cycles: Monarch
Butterfly

metamorphosis ..... changing,
developing
milkweed .... plant, green
consumer .... eater
splits .... breaks, opens
weeks .... months, days
chrysalis .... cocoon, dormant
repeats .... restarts, continues

- High-frequency words: **belong, butterfly, through, non-stop, eggshell, until, changing, two, repeats**
- Content specific words: **flutter, monarch butterfly, metamorphosis, milkweed, larva, non-stop food consumer, molting, changing skin, chrysalis, stage, immobile**

Pages C-D—Life Cycles: Green Snake

terrified .... frightened, amazed
fascinating .... amazing, interesting
male .... female, male
leathery .... hard, rough
cutting .... breaking, cracking
molting .... leaving, shedding
protecting .... covering, around
scales .... scales
camouflage .... coloring
clear .... special, unique
forked .... pronged
swallowing .... eating, devouring,
consuming

- High-frequency words: **wriggle, overlapping, unnoticed, people, describe**
- Content specific words: **terrified, response, fascinating, meadow, mating, leathery, eggshells, wriggle, molting, protecting, overlapping scales, camouflage, enemies, forked tongue, detects odors, unique**

Pages E-F—Newspapers

project .... unit, activity
national .... international,
worldwide
reporter .... writer, journalist
different .... unique, special
condense .... fit, shorten
promotions .... specials, sales
publish .... write, create
suggestions .... advice, solutions
horoscopes .... advertisements, want
ads

- High-frequency words: **stories, usually, include, expires, shorthand, purchase, decided, situation, suggestions, favorites**
- Content specific words: **newspaper project, national interest, reporter, byline, advertisements, abbreviations, advertisers, condense information, promotions, consumers, publish, advice columns, sports section, horoscope, comics, entertainment section**

Pages G-H—Walt Disney

brainstorms .... ideas, inspirations
presentation .... report, speech
memorized .... learned, recited
principal .... teacher, librarian
features .... includes, spotlights
project .... assignment,
presentation
famous .... important, known
rejected .... eliminated, scorned
negative .... unkind, bad, poor
memorable .... special, unique

- High-frequency words: **people, projects, assignment, headed, homemade, outstanding, throughout, features, originated**
- Content specific words: **brainstorms, Disneyland®, assignment, oral presentation, memorized, Lincoln's Gettysburg Address, animated, outstanding, principal, Hall of Presidents, attraction, rejected, negative evaluation, memorable moments**

Pages I-J—Johnny Appleseed

legends .... myths, heroes
flashback .... retelling
leased .... shared, rented
seeding .... planting, starting
doubled .... doubled, served
welcomed .... greeted, enjoyed
vinegar .... juice
barter .... trade, exchange
Revolutionary .... Revolutionary
respect .... love, concern

- High-frequency words: **created, died, owned, leased, wherever, welcomed**
- Content specific words: **legends, bigger than life, flashback, leased, Ohio Valley, seeding apple orchards, settlers, vinegar, barter, preservative, pelts, orphaned, respect, Revolutionary War, burlap sack**

Bibliography of Children's Works

Guess the covered word.

Because Brian Hugged His Mother by David L. Rice (Dawn Publications, 1999).

Life Cycles: Green Snake by David M. Schwartz and Dwight Kuhn (Creative Teaching Press, 1999).

Life Cycles: Monarch Butterfly by David M. Schwartz and Dwight Kuhn (Creative Teaching Press, 1999).

Lifetimes by David L. Rice (Dawn Publications, 1997).

Littlejim's Gift: An Appalachian Christmas Story by Gloria Houston (The Putnam & Grosset Group, 1998).

The Magic School Bus: At the Waterworks by Joanna Cole (Scholastic, 1988).

Mufaro's Beautiful Daughters: An African Tale by John Steptoe (Lothrop, Lee & Shepard Books, 1987).

Stone Fox by John Reynolds Gardiner (HarperTrophy, 1980).

Yeh-Shen: A Cinderella Story from China by Ai-Ling Louie (Puffin Books, 1974).